VOICES

A COACHING STORY TO
INSPIRE YOUR FUTURE

BY AILEEN GIBB

Copyright © 2013 by Aileen Gibb
First Edition – April 2013

ISBN
978-1-4602-1723-8 (Hardcover)
978-1-4602-1724-5 (Paperback)
978-1-4602-1725-2 (eBook)

Produced by:

FriesenPress
Suite 300 – 852 Fort Street
Victoria, BC, Canada V8W 1H8

www.friesenpress.com

Distributed to the trade by The Ingram Book Company

"Aileen Gibb's beautifully-written, interwoven stories on the power of questions had a profound impact on me. I relate to the guide who fights against simple solutions - to sit quietly, look within and seek my own answers. As I read, I saw that life can be as simple as I choose to make it. As I witnessed each character open up to this possibility and transform their lives, I felt encouraged about the possibilities in my own life." (Linda Dessau, Content Mastery Guide)

"This book had me intrigued and wanting more. I loved gathering with the characters in anticipation of where they would go and what they would uncover next. As well as being an interesting story, this book encourages reflection and stimulates possibilities and is a great coaching tool professionally or personally." (Barbara Watt, Chicago)

"I love the Fable format which teaches without preaching. The circle conversation, mixed with the personal stories, works very well. Each left me wanting more, not necessarily from the book, but in a conversation. This is an excellent tool for coaching clients, opening the door for more learning. Reads like a lovely tale while offering important lessons." (Betty Healey, The roadSigns Coach)

for Fawna

This book is dedicated to the voices of the many
inspired clients, colleagues, coaches and friends,
who add immeasurable value to my own journey.

May you continue to claim fully, all that your life can be.

This book was inspired by a question. One question from a coaching colleague inspired me to commit to a daily writing practice.

I wanted to write about the powerful world of questions and to share stories of what can happen when you respond. I did not know what shape this would take as a book. I trusted that the question was leading me somewhere. It was a magical experience to sit down each day and watch the characters develop, to see the connections between them appear and to experience the unfolding of Tashia's vision for the future.

VOICES emerged.

My hope is that you connect with at least one of the stories. You may find one that mirrors a decision or a choice you currently face, or you may hear one question calling you so strongly that you know you have to explore and answer it.

Time and again a coaching conversation, with the right questions, will take you somewhere you didn't realize you were ready to go. Tashia represents the inner voice that seeks to guide you and which, when heard fully, opens up magical possibilities. As you listen and find your answers, may life, in Tashia's words, become all you claim it to be.

With gratitude for the questions waiting to be heard.

Prologue

May life bring all you wish for.
I am Tashia: river of your soul,
earth of your spirit,
air of your voice
and fire of your being.
I am the infinite space of your possibility.

I am the voice of the questions that beg your response.
I am Tashia: may you claim fully all that your life can be.

It is a time for trust.
You may not know it yet. In time you will.
You will feel it in each inspired moment.
Growing eventually to embrace life in the new community.

ONE
Tashia

Tashia puts her trust in the rotting wooden bridge that carries her back from the ancient circle, whose stones she often visits after a hectic day at work. The ageless, battle-scarred stones listen well to her frustration and understand her concern that the company is heading for disaster. She is convinced there must be another way. She's had weeks to get her recommendations in, and now, with only twenty-four hours to the board meeting, she still isn't sure what she will say.

The mountain peaks stand out against northern sky. Evening sunbeams reach down to play with her as she clicks the automatic start button on her Volkswagen key. The doors unlock to receive her. She has walked barefoot across the cool grass of dusk, and she throws the light sandals she carries onto the back seat then slips in behind the steering wheel and closes her eyes. She feels safe here, safe and secure from the stresses she faces daily. She lets go of the breath she'd been holding, releasing the energy of the standing stones so that it might travel with her in her modern-day chariot.

She wonders again if it had been a real voice she heard as she sat within the ancient circle. The voice had pierced her to the core and frightened her with its request.

"I am Ghoy," said the voice. *A strange name*, she thinks.

"And I speak to you, Tashia, on behalf of the council of Future Guides. We need you to build a new community. How we once ruled no longer fits the need. We must start anew and lay a new foundation. We must learn new ways. This is your purpose, Tashia. This is the task for which you have been chosen. There are no guidelines. Travel, Tashia, to discover what people need, and then let us know how best to respond."

Tashia shakes her head clear of the message, which had been pounding at her temples all the way back down the path. *What does it mean?*

All she has gathered from her business travels in the past five years are questions. Questions that have helped many people make a difference in their lives. Yet, how would she turn these into guidance for a new community? So far, most people she meets are skeptical that asking questions and allowing people to find their own answers can help them solve their organizational woes. And yet, they keep asking her for more questions.

Before she knows it, she turns into the drive of the house she and her husband had designed and built only three years ago. As she hears his voice, belting out his own version of Pavarotti through the open kitchen window, she smiles, diverted for the moment from the voice in the stones. Smiling, she opens the car door, steps onto the gravel drive and runs up the steps, letting all worries from her business day take a back seat. Dan's voice is one she knows and has confidence in. Dan, she knows, will listen.

In no time, she is curled up on the sofa, a plate of pasta balanced on her knee; she is listening to Dan's day and putting her own out of mind.

It is Dan's snoring that jolts her awake some hours later. Tashia rises and walks through the open French doors onto the late evening patio, where she is embraced by the orange glow of an oversized harvest moon.

TWO
The Circle

The proud circle of stones resonates with the voices of the Future Guides, in the still night air of summer. Tashia feels the energy of the moon behind her, and she seems to float over the ancient bridge, crossing the mountain stream as it merges with the lakeshore. As she steps through the gate, onto the summer dew, she is filled with joy. For in this moment, all she works for, all she believes in and all she wishes for, comes true.

The ancient stone circle has something, possibly everything, to do with it.

She feels the stones reach across the land. The mountain peaks are clearly outlined against the late dusk of a northern July. Stars reach down to play with her. Her heart expands with her love of this land, welcoming its regeneration after years of

5

harsh, shortsighted destruction, which engulfed it as she grew up. This is her home. She always comes back. She feels safe here. She has witnessed sights of pain and destruction. Ghoy had said it would be so. Now her hope is to see a new community created for the future. This, she senses, is why the Guides have invited her to the circle tonight.

She turns instinctively towards Ghoy. He nods and invites her to take her seat amongst the stones. "Welcome back, Tashia." Ghoy's words startle her with their warmth, and she shivers at the contrast with the cool night. His simple words eat into the core of her being, as if they are already inside her. She knows tonight will give her the strength she needs. She waits in silence.

"I speak to you, Tashia, on behalf of the council of Future Guides," he says. Vibrant energy radiates through her whole being. Something important is imminent. She stills the faint fear that stirs within her and concentrates on Ghoy's words. "The Future Guides have been discussing how best to move forward with the new community. It would seem we are undecided. It seems—"

"It is easy." A dark-cowled Guide to Tashia's left interrupts Ghoy. "We know the rules need to be set out. Let's get on with it. Tell people what they need to do, and make sure there are penalties if they fail to follow the rules."

Murmurs of disagreement are heard around the circle of Guides.

"We need to follow the plan we set out last season," shouts another Guide from the back of the circle. "It's easy. Just repeat what we know. It has worked before."

A sigh is heard from Ghoy's right. A figure materializes: The Convener—though Tashia could not say how she knew his title. He turns to Ghoy and asks, in a voice intended for the entire circle, "Ghoy, why is it you have brought Tashia here tonight? What are you proposing we do?"

With an encouraging glance at Tashia, Ghoy addresses the circle. His voice is deep and solid, carrying an air of trust that quickly silences his peers.

"It seems to me that the ways of before are not what we are looking for now." His voice is confident. "If we are to create a new community, then we must start from new beginnings, with new assumptions. We must learn new ways to relate and com-municate with each other. This will be an experiment. There are no guidelines, other than what I suspect lies within all our hearts, if only we would allow it to guide us. It is for this chal-lenge that we have been chosen as the Future Guides. Yet, even we appear to be caught up in our attachments to past ways of doing things. It is for this reason that I have invited Tashia. She brings a new perspective from her many travels around our earth, and I invite you now to consider her proposal. Tashia?"

She walks hesitatingly to the centre of the gathering and lays a circle of brightly-coloured cards around her. "I invite each of you to select and read a card," she says.

The Guides comply.

"My card is a question," shouts the dark-cowled Guide.

"As is mine."

"And mine."

"There are no proposals here," says another. "How can questions alone create the future?"

Tashia feels their impatience.

"One moment," she pleads, "these are questions gathered from my travels. These questions help people in times of confusion and challenge. Allow me to continue my travels and to build on these questions. From these will come our guidance for the new community. There is power in asking questions that have not been asked before. And there is much joy and fulfillment in listening as people find their own answers."

"Find their own answers?" The dark-cowled Guide is incredulous. "What nonsense. It is our job to create the plan for the future. We hold the answers within our knowledge and experience. That is why we are chosen as the Guides."

"I don't doubt that you are chosen as Guides because you each have much to offer. It is the manner in which those gifts are shared with others that is key."

"What is it you need, Tashia?" asks Ghoy.

"I need only your blessing to continue with my travels. To be free to inspire whoever needs a question to further their path."

Ghoy, turning to the circle of Guides asks on her behalf. "Do you give Tashia your support? Do you have the courage to explore this new way?"

Around the circle, the Guides nod slowly, one by one. All, except the dark-cowled Guide, who remains skeptical.

"Then, with this agreement, go forward, Tashia. We have but one request of you. You are invited to the circle each full moon to share your learning with us. Bring us the powerful questions *you discover. It would appear that we, too, need to learn from them. Let us work together to gather their power for the future."*

"Thank you, Ghoy," says Tashia. "I will do my best."

As she leaves, a new sense of purpose passes through her like a pulse of energy. Her mission is clear. She is grateful for the loving support of Ghoy and the Future Guides. Quietly she knows that what she brings back will be of great value to them. She sighs deeply as she moves through the outer stones of the circle to continue her mission in this saddened, crying land.

THREE
Samuel

Samuel jolts awake as his car wheel bumps the kerb. Panicking, he slams on the brake and comes to a halt on the grass verge. He rubs his eyes and his throbbing temples. Louis Armstrong's "What a Wonderful World" mocks him through the radio speakers. He lets exhaustion and his leaden eyelids take over. He could sleep right here and now. He waits for his heartbeat to settle, looking out at the children's playground on his left. He glimpses the silhouette of a woman against the orange moon which hangs low in the sky.

As he steps on the grass, Samuel ignores the dampness dulling his shiny black Gucci shoes. The swings, where he has laughed many times with his son and daughter, circle around him. He squeezes into a faded red plastic seat, clenching the chains designed for much smaller fists. Rusty brackets strain under his weight as he replays the phone conversation he just had with Jayne. The disappointment in his wife's voice tugs at him.

"When will you be home?" she'd hissed. He knew it pointless to blame the urgency of the Colombian sales contract again. Jayne had given up any interest in the details of his work. *Maybe when this contract is put to bed, things will change*, he thinks. *I'll get my next promotion. The new house will make us happy again.*

"I'll leave in twenty minutes," he'd offered. An already failed promise, as he simultaneously scanned more email. "Yes, yes," he'd placated. "I'll be home before they are asleep." He wasn't. And now he is here, swinging to and fro, wondering why.

He hears a voice in his head: *What is it that you want from life, Samuel Jones? What will make you happy?*

These were questions which had been interrupting his planning on the Colombian contract. He had ignored them— or tried to. Now the evening seems to stand still, expecting a long overdue answer.

The silhouetted woman settles herself on the bark-covered ground. Intended to protect young limbs from cuts and grazes, tonight it serves as a comfortable cushion on the damp earth. Samuel seems, somehow, to know her. He watches her lay brightly-coloured cards on the ground, catching one back from the dance of the evening breeze.

"What are you doing?" asks Samuel, intrigued.

"That may be a question to ask yourself, Samuel," she responds. Her voice has an unusual ring to it. Melodic, it reaches compassionately inside him.

"How happy are you with life, Samuel? What's happened to your dreams?"

Samuel hesitates to speak aloud the answers screaming inside him. For if he keeps them to himself, he doesn't have to act on them, surely.

"Are you ready to hear yourself?" the woman's voice seems to shine out of the darkness, piercing him deep in the chest.

Samuel surprises himself: "Yes, I know it's time. I am not happy. I am worried about Jayne. We used to have time as a family. We'd go sailing. Now all I do is work."

"What would you rather have?"

His reply comes quickly: "I want this Colombian contract closed out. I want to get back to spending my weekends with Jayne and the kids. I am under such pressure to get this deal done. It's a crucial part of next year's budget. The deadline is three months away yet. I don't know if I can hold on to Jayne for that long."

"How do you feel about that?"

A heavy despair swallows him. "I can't let that happen. I'm only doing this work to provide the life Jayne and I want for the kids. I'm scared of letting them all down. I've got to push ahead with it."

"Let's imagine, Samuel, you can create anything you want for yourself. What would be happening right now?"

The questions intertwine with Samuel's thoughts, like a movie scene playing out in his head.

"I imagine myself at the office. Jayne comes to pick me up. The kids are waiting in the car. We are off to the coast. As I leave the office, my phone rings. Dan, our CEO, is calling me to say the Colombian deal has been signed. I can forget about it and enjoy my family time. I'm looking forward to the sailing and to water games with the kids. I switch off my mobile phone, close down my laptop and leave them in the office. My assistant, Paul, assures me he can handle things for the next week. I am on holiday."

"Are you ready to do that?"

"Nowhere near it. I don't have holiday time booked. I'm scared to add any more to Paul's workload. Jayne and I let our membership at the sailing club lapse. Dan is constantly on my back about the contract. I can't do it. I just can't see any way out." Samuel shakes his head. "This contract is too important to everyone."

"Well, let's imagine it to be possible. What would be your first step?"

"I'd take a day off and just relax with the kids, but as I say, the contract is too imp—"

"Which day would you take off?"

"Well, I guess I'd take Friday off so that we had some weekend time, but—"

"Your *but* is getting in the way Samuel," the voice says with a light laugh. "Will you give up saying *but* just for the moment?"

"Well, yes, b— oh I see what you mean. I say 'but' and am looking for an excuse, before I even consider what could be possible."

"Thank you. Now where were we?"

"I was saying that I would like to take next Friday off, to have a long weekend with my family and give myself a break from the contract."

"Thank you. You already sound more positive. How might you make this happen?"

Samuel sighs and considers the question. The swing twists back as he releases it, jumping to the ground.

"Of course it's possible. The draft contract is submitted on Wednesday, and then we have to wait for the client's response. I was going to clear my backlog of paperwork for the rest of the week, but that can wait. I can ask Paul to help me with it. Wow, I believe there is nothing to stop me taking Friday off."

"I wish you well with your dreams, Samuel."

The voice fades to a whisper as Samuel turns towards his car again. Intent on his plans for the weekend, he doesn't see the woman's reflection bounce off his car. He doesn't notice the coloured cards scattered on the passenger seat as he turns on the ignition and heads for home. The voice may be coming from his radio, or carrying on the late evening breeze:

My name is Tashia. May life bring all you wish for.

...all you wish for. The words come back to Samuel as he trims the sails on Serendipity to catch the early autumn breeze blowing across the lake. Satisfied that they are on course, he ties off the lanyard and settles down again by Jayne, stretched

out on the deck. He takes the glass of red wine she pours for him.

"To us and all we wish for," he says quietly, moving beyond the ritual clinking of the glasses to kiss her gently on the lips he'd been missing for too long now.

"I'll drink to that," she says.

"I'm so glad we did this." He pulls her back down on the Burberry check blanket. "Mmmm... so good."

"Well, I don't know what took you so long," murmurs Jayne, untangling the wind knots in her hair with her fingers. "But I'm certainly glad you arranged all this on such short notice. The kids have had a great day. It's so long since we've had this good a time. Has your headache cleared up?"

"It's well gone," replies Samuel. "I guess it was just the stress I've been under. I was pretty close to heading to the surgery to see what Doc Green thought. He'd probably have had me in for a brain scan before I knew it. All I needed was some down time. Imagine that."

"Is that what scared you into taking this time off?" Jayne asks, probing his mind as her gloved fingers squeeze the well-toned arm muscles through his windbreaker. She'd forgotten how good it was to be together.

"I think if I'd done this because I was scared of something, I wouldn't be having so much fun. Just take it from me: I'm here because I want to be and because I realize how important you are to me. To be honest, I'm surprised you didn't walk out on me before now. I couldn't have stood that. I love you and the kids, and that's what makes the work worthwhile. I'm sorry I haven't been around enough."

"It's fine," says Jayne, closing her eyes and pulling the blanket around her shoulders, as if the shiver came from the breeze and not the thought of how close she'd come to doing just that. "We've got a lot going for us, and now that we're getting a chance to remind ourselves of that, I for one, am in for the long haul."

"Me too," says Samuel, "and speaking about long hauls, I think we're probably far enough out. I better get us back to port. Come join me at the wheel."

Resuming control of the vessel they'd hired for the weekend, Samuel hums gently to disguise the conversation going on in his head.

He remembers Tashia's voice and how she had pushed him gently through his fears and objections. Without it, he might have talked himself out of this weekend and put the company before his family again. Thankfully, his commitment was strong enough to overcome anything else that could have got in his way. The company would win in the long run, for he would return refreshed and energized—confident in his relationship, relaxed and healthy. He'd sail through the contract details now and couldn't wait to see what life had in store when he was out the other side of it again. More moments with Jayne like this would certainly be worth it.

Again he hears the wind whisper to him:

Well done, Samuel. May life be all you claim it to be.

FOUR
Awareness

Tashia steps through the sunset, into the circle of Guides. She feels Ghoy's welcome and at the same time catches the frown of the dark-cowled Guide. She settles down in the middle of the circle and relates the story of Samuel. She lays out some new coloured cards and lays a purple stone on top of them to keep them still.

"How many people do you meet with a story similar to Samuel's?" asks Ghoy.

"I have met many. It's what may be destroying this land and its people," says Tashia. "People are unaware of what is happening. They believe themselves to be servants of huge, complex systems. They forget who they are. They don't ask questions

about what is important to them. They think this is progress. They think this is success. They forget why they are here."

"How might the new community learn from this?" asks Ghoy, contemplatively rubbing his chin.

"The learning lies in questions." Tashia sees the dark-cowled Guide turn away impatiently. She carries on. "People need to be more aware of their current situation; to ask themselves: 'When did I last slow down, take time for myself and look at what is important to me in my life?'"

"Let those questions be recorded." With a flourish of his left hand, Ghoy invites the Scribe to preserve Tashia's words.

"We may also wish to guide people to breathe more healthily," suggests Tashia.

"Humphh!" The dark-cowled Guide is indignant. "I think we have more important things to do than teach people to breathe. That comes naturally, doesn't it?"

"That's true of course. Yet I meet many people in my travels whose breathing seems laboured. It is fast and shallow. They feel stress. Breath provides us with fuel for our bodies and our minds. Many breathe in toxic air as the world falls apart around them. The air in the new community will be clean. We must encourage people to breathe it in again, slowly and deeply, to provide them with the energy and clarity they need. Everyone must take time to breathe life in more fully." Tashia draws a deep breath of night air.

"Once people are breathing again," she says, "we can teach them to take time for quality conversations such as the one I just

had with Samuel. Well-intentioned questions will help anyone to see things more clearly and with a different perspective."

"What do you mean by a well-intentioned question?" asks Ghoy.

"Well, the most interesting thing I've discovered about questions," says Tashia with a soft laugh, "is that I don't always know where they come from. When I focus on listening to what the other person is saying or experiencing—and I mean being present to what the situation means for them—I find that my questions come to me. Maybe they come from within me. Maybe they come from somewhere bigger than me (she looks sneakily at Ghoy as if to suggest he has been somehow prompting her questions) or maybe they come from the other person. When my intention is to be fully attentive to the other person and to be of service to them, then the most amazing questions emerge from my lips.

"The most powerful questions are often the ones the other person doesn't ask of themselves. I only hear those questions when I create a deep connection, through listening to what is happening in that person's life or work. In those moments, I ask the questions only because I truly want the other person to find their own answers, not because I want to give them the answer or because I want them to do what I think is the right thing to do."

"Is this something anyone can do?" asks Ghoy.

"It takes deep listening to hear and ask the most powerful questions of another person. It takes courage to overcome the fear that this question might hurt or offend them. It takes

trust and a strong belief that the question will help the other person. This trust only comes if the intention is to serve and care for others."

"I ask again whether this is something anyone can do?" Ghoy is insistent.

"Anyone can learn to do this if they are prepared to change the way they look at the world. I have heard many stories of this land where people, sadly, did not take time for each other. I constantly heard them trying to prove that their view of the world was right and everyone else was wrong." Tashia notices that the dark-cowled Guide has left the circle.

"They were judging others and trying to prove themselves all the time. I came across no one with this approach who had the ability to ask powerful, helpful questions. My point is, that in order to truly appreciate the value of another person, I have first learned to stand in their shoes and seek to understand what is important to them and to appreciate how the world looks through their eyes. It was not easy for me to do so. I found my own experiences often interfered with my questions to others. So I taught myself to put my own views, assumptions, experiences and opinions aside until I helped the other uncover what is within them. I do this by imagining I have a large basket into which I can temporarily pack all my own thoughts and views. I quickly discovered so much more about what was within the other person. Often they had all the answers they needed. They simply needed to ask the right questions."

"What would you call this learning?"

"I'd like to call it Awareness. Awareness of our own behaviours, responses, judgments and perspectives. Until we become aware of something, by stopping to look at it and then to reflect on it, we can bring no hope of change to this land."

"How do we bring people to awareness?" Ghoy asks.

"I'm not sure we can bring awareness to everyone, particularly anyone who does not wish to look at how they are living their life." Tashia cannot help but look around for the dark-cowled Guide.

"For those who are willing, we can act like a mirror. We can become an extension of the other person. In Samuel's case, for example, I heard him replay our conversation while he continued his drive home. He said it was as if he had another pair of eyes to see himself with; another pair of ears to listen with and hear what's going on inside him as well as on the surface. He felt he had a new voice to help him express things he might not otherwise express, in language he didn't even know he could use, or questions he was afraid to ask himself. Somehow he was able to access a part of himself he didn't normally use; a part that opens up new ideas and possibilities. It's like part of his inner spirit, allowing him to feel, experience and understand things normally kept hidden. This gives a new strength to explore pathways never before explored."

Tashia laughs to herself. "I guess Samuel might have thought of it as another part of his engine, which kicked him into high gear and provided the power, energy and clarity for him to move towards a future he wants. He certainly became much more aware of himself and his current situation, and then he took action to change it."

"And you say this is all because of the questions, which you have now captured on these cards before us?" asks the Convenor, as he joins Tashia in the circle to study the cards more closely.

"Well, yes," she says, hanging on to her belief in what she had experienced. "I've come to believe that questions have the power to serve others in a new way. We have been missing this understanding. Questions can guide people on a journey of discovery and help them find new ways to live. Is that not what you seek for the future community?"

"Yes, it may be," say the Convenor. He is intrigued by Tashia's conviction and wants to hear more. "Please continue."

Tashia notices he is still holding the cards in his hands.

"As I travel, I observe that much of the time the people I meet do not pay attention to what is going on around them and how they are responding to it. They follow the patterns they inherited from those who went before them. They deny themselves the opportunity to fully experience their life as it is right now, in this moment. They don't realize that this may be all there is. This moment may be the most important in their life, and they might miss it.

"Questions help people to slow down, like Samuel did, and to become aware of why they respond to situations in a certain way."

"Is there a secret to asking the right questions, then?" asks Ghoy, standing over the shoulder of the Scribe, continually urging him to capture all the details of Tashia's discoveries.

"I don't consider it a secret, more of a skill. The more our new community can ask questions in this way, the more hope there will be of success within that community."

"So what are the key skills of good questioning?"

"Firstly, good questions come from true listening. There is no one set of 'right' questions that work for everyone. The clues to the right questions are in the other person's words, actions and feelings. To truly listen, we use all our senses to hear what is happening for the other person. Beyond our obvious five senses, we have an innate ability to perceive things in more subtle ways. These ways have been neglected in the community of old, and yet they offer us an opportunity to see and understand so much more about ourselves and others. My wish for the new community is that we learn to combine our more subtle senses and truly open up to increased awareness of ourselves and others. Without this, I fear the new community will remain immune to the true possibilities within it. Imagine, that by simply tuning in to the other person with our full range of senses, we find the clues to ask what they need to ask of themselves."

Tashia realizes that the circle has gone very quiet around her. "Am I talking too much?" she asks. "Is this what you want to hear?"

The Convenor settles back into his chair. "With the exception of our dark-cowled colleague, my sense is that you are sharing exactly what we need to hear. Do we want Tashia to continue?" he asks, addressing the circle with a wide sweep of his hand.

"Yes."

"Yes, please continue."

"Thank you," says Tashia. "I feel very well listened to, here in the circle. We must encourage our new community to also attend to their listening ability.

"I hear many people claim to be good listeners, but the evidence I have gathered on my travels suggests otherwise. Often, it appears to me they are just waiting for the other person to stop talking, so that they can inject their own thoughts, ideas, suggestions and answers into the conversation. All the time, people claim the conversation for themselves. They are so anxious to tell their story that they do not create listening space for others.

"I have learned that, in order to truly listen, I need first to silence all the voices inside me. I put aside my own desire to be heard. I hold on to my own suggestions, even if they come from my real experiences. My biggest challenge has been to give up the need to 'fix things' for the other person. To be right. To have all the answers.

"When I do this, then the most magical things happen. It creates space for the other person to reflect, to explore, to enquire, to discover their own possibilities. And in turn I have so often learned from them. This is what I mean by true listening."

"The first step to effective questions, therefore, is true listening." says Ghoy.

"Yes. Next, it is important that your questions guide the other person towards future solutions. This land has died because too much energy was drained by conversations stuck in the past, where people go over the same ground again and again, not saying anything new. I have seen many gatherings where little *is accomplished or achieved because no one knows how to ask questions that move people into the future."*

"What type of questions might help them?" asks Ghoy, knowingly.

"Questions that are future focused such as 'What do you want to be happening? What will it take to move forward or change? What's possible?' We need to look out for people who are stuck in the problem, like Samuel, and can't stand back to see a way forward."

Tashia is aware of the dark-cowled Guide as he re-enters the circle and approaches the Convenor. "I fail to see how all this talk of questions is leading to a plan for the new community," he says. "I think it time we moved on to more productive things."

Tashia approaches. "Would you be willing to engage in further conversation with me?" she asks gently of the dark-cowled Guide. "Perhaps you will allow me to explore the power of questions with you?"

The dark-cowled Guide hesitates and looks appealingly at the Convenor. "Yes," says the Convenor unexpectedly, "I like this idea. It will let us see for real what Tashia is talking about. Come, Guide, help us by participating in this exchange with her."

Tashia invites the dark-cowled Guide to sit by her, as the rest of the circle settle once again to listen.

"What do you need from this conversation?" Tashia asks.

The Convenor edges forward ready to interrupt. He had expected Tashia to lead off by convincing the dark-cowled Guide he needed to listen to her. He stops himself just in time, opening to the possibility of something new taking place before him.

"What will make this a worthwhile conversation for you?"

The dark-cowled Guide also hesitates in surprise. Her questions have made him stop and think. He is not used to such an approach. "Well," he says, aware of his discomfort. "I need to know what you know. What is this stuff about questions that you are talking about?"

"What makes that important to you?" asks Tashia.

"It's very important. We are here as the circle of Guides for the future community. We can't afford to waste our time on things that might not be helping us move forward with the creation of that community."

"What do you want to see happening? How will you know when that new community has been created?" Tashia sits comfortably in silence awaiting his response.

"I want a community where people are collaborating. Creating new ways to live, work and produce together. I want a community where things work smoothly. I want a community where peace is more important than war and where we are proud to live together and help each other," he says. "Is that too much to ask for?"

Tashia smiles. "That's not for me to say. I am sure you can have whatever you wish. How near to that picture do you feel you currently are?"

"Well, the citizens are getting together regularly for planning meetings. This council is meeting regularly. We've studied

four blueprints so far. Things are moving forward. Lots of people are doing lots of things to help."

"And what about you? How close to that desired picture of community are you?" asks Tashia.

"Me? Why do you ask about me? The community is what is important—surely you can see that?"

"Who do you mean by the community?"

"I mean all of us. I mean you, me, all the other Guides here."

"I hear you say you are part of that community," she says. "May I ask you again how close to that desired picture you yourself are at this time?"

"Well, for the most part, I live life as I wish. I have the odd argument here and there. I can't stand wasting time on useless ideas. But overall I am committed to being part of that new community," he says. "Why do you ask about me?"

"Why do you think I ask about you? Please take some time to think about it." Tashia is patient and still.

The Guides in the circle watch the dark-cowled one with deep interest. They sense something is shifting within him. He has calmed down. His frustration is lessening. He is almost unaware of the circle, as he carefully considers his next response to Tashia's questions.

Tashia gauges her next question carefully. She considers whether it needs to be asked. Her intuition tells her to go ahead. It is the question the Guide needs to hear.

"What is your role in the new community?" she asks and waits again. The silence is clear and open, without the fearful energy often felt when no one speaks.

"My role is to lead the community to a new future, along with my colleagues in the circle here. I am proud to be part of that transition. It is an honour to be part of the new path."

"What will make your role successful for you?"

"Why, all the things I've already said."

"I believe what you told me before were all the things that will make the future successful for the community," she says. "May I ask you to consider what it will mean for you personally?"

Again the Guide takes some time to respond. Tashia can almost hear the thinking and the emotions moving within him. Again, she holds the silence.

"I want to be remembered as part of the change," the Guide declares at last. "That will make it successful for me. I want to leave something for the next generation."

"So now, help me understand what you need from this conversation."

"I want to know how to carry out my role in helping create the new community in a way that means I will have left something meaningful for the next generation." exclaims the Guide, and his cowl slips from his head as he jumps up in response to the muted cheer coming from the circle around him.

Tashia can see the new light in his eyes, and she smiles. "How do you feel at this moment?"

"Why, I am seeing my role in a new light. I'm feeling excited about it. Can't wait to move on, in fact, which brings me back to wanting to move on with things around here."

"Would you be willing to think about one more question?"

"Okay, then," he says, "what is it?"

"Can you reflect on our conversation and tell me what I did that helped you get this new feeling?"

"Well, we just talked, didn't we?" A faint hint of his earlier frustration returning.

"Did we?" asks Tashia. "What exactly did I do? How exactly did I talk?"

"Oh, I see how you've tricked me. You asked me lots of questions, didn't you?"

Tashia refrains from replying. "Did it help you in any way?"

"Yes. I can see things very differently," he says. "I feel different. I sense I am part of the circle again. I want to listen to more of this conversation now. In fact, I might even be beginning to think it will help us move into the future."

"Why do you think that is?" asks Tashia, encouraging the Guide to reflect further on this experience.

"Your questions unlocked something within me. I feel like I've got a new energy and that it's leading me in a new direction. I was starting to feel I needed to move away from the circle. Now I feel part of it again. That's powerful."

"Did I hear you say powerful? What's powerful?"

"Those questions you asked," says the Guide, before he realizes what he has said.

Several quiet smiles lighten the mood around the circle, as more than the dark-cowled Guide have come to understand the potential of the questions Tashia has asked. If such questions can shift the heart of a Guide as set in the old ways as this one, then perhaps they do carry some answers for the future.

Tashia looks to the sky where the black profile of the moun-
tains is starting to glow pink with the early sun. She hurries
to place the purple stone in the centre of the circle and pulls
another from the deep pocket of her robe.

"These stones are taken from the lands of my journeys,"
she says.

"Let the first be a reminder for us not to be prisoners of our
current reality; a reminder that, however trapped we may feel,
there is a powerful question which can unlock our new path.

"Let the second stone, this earth-brown pebble, represent the
value of self-awareness that is within our reach and can lead us
to new learning."

As the circle of Guides start to depart, Ghoy and the Convenor
approach Tashia. "Well, my dear, where are you going to travel
to next? What further treasures will you bring back to us?"

"Oh, I think I know where to go now. Samuel has a friend
and co-worker..."

FIVE
Paul

Samuel bounds up the office steps and into his office. Paul, his assistant, ignores his "Good morning" as well as the double latte and cinnamon bun he sets down on the spreadsheets Paul is engrossed in. "These are for you," says Samuel.

"Huh," grunts Paul, "it's going to take more than a coffee to make up for leaving me with Dan on Friday. You obviously had a good weekend."

"Yep," says Samuel, refusing to be drawn into Paul's mood. "What's up with you? Dan been on your case again?"

"And then some. I nearly walked out on Friday, Colombian contract or not. I'm used to last-minute meetings, but let's face it, calling one at four on a Friday afternoon and keeping us trapped till nine o'clock is too much. I was seething inside and missed my dinner with Claire. And what did we gain? Nothing, as far as I can see. He insisted on going over the projections again; maybe he wasn't listening when we did that last Tuesday. All because he hadn't prepared his client presentation for this morning. Now I'm behind with these spreadsheets. Sometimes that guy is just too much.

"How long will it take you to finish these?" asks Samuel. It's too easy to waste time complaining about Dan; if they start down that road, no work will get done before lunchtime. Somewhere in the back of Samuel's mind a voice calls for his attention.

"Accounts need them by noon. Go away and let me get on with it." Paul grabs the now cold latte, and curses as it spills onto his spreadsheets. "Look, will you please just go away?"

"Okay, okay, I only want to help," says Samuel. "How about we bunk off for a couple of hours at lunchtime and chat about it. I'll buy."

"Call me at noon and I'll see. Now get out…"

At five minutes to twelve, Paul feels Samuel's hand on his shoulder. "Okay, we're getting out of here. Come on, here's your coat."

"But…" Paul starts to protest then shakes his head. He had intended to check the spreadsheets one more time. Reluctantly, he presses send on the email and hopes for the best. His mood hasn't improved. "Where are we going anyway? What's the rush? Don't we have to be back in an hour?"

Samuel shrugs and laughs. "I don't know that we have to do anything to please anyone else," he says. "That's why I want to chat with you. I have some learning to share with you. I promise it will help you."

It's a warm autumn day outside, with an occasional passing cloud to block the heat from the sun. Otherwise, it's warm enough to sit in the open air and wonder how the moon can be seen so clearly during the day. At the sandwich bar, waiting for their order, Samuel whistles to himself as Paul looks out from under angry, tired brows. He wonders how Samuel can be so jaunty at such a crucial stage of the contract.

They make their way to the quadrangle behind the imposing glass and steel structure of the IF-Q building where, moments before, they were at their desks. They grab a free bench by the circular fountain. Samuel notices the shadow of a woman sitting on the far side of the cascading spray of water. He senses something familiar about her as he turns his attention to Paul.

"So what's up?" Samuel asks. "I'm listening."

"That's more than anyone else is doing in this company," says Paul, unwrapping his BLT and popping open his root beer. "I'm tired of being treated like a spare part. I made a couple of great suggestions last week for speeding up the project. Dan promised to look at them, but it seems to me that he probably threw them in the waste bin. He doesn't think I have anything worthwhile to offer. I might as well be a cardboard cut-out for all the notice he takes of my ideas. I don't know that I want to work like this. I struggle to come to the office each morning. I hate it."

"You sound pretty worked up about this," says Samuel patiently.

"It's not about me. It's Dan's style of management. I'm fed up with it."

"That's what I mean; there's a lot going on inside you. All you can talk about is how you feel about Dan and this place." It's a familiar pattern to Samuel. He's seen Paul act like this before when things don't go his way.

"And since when do my feelings matter?" Paul asks defensively.

"It matters to me," Samuel says. "We've worked together for a long time. I enjoy working with you, not to mention the times we play tennis together. I don't like to see you impacted by Dan in this way. You don't have to put up with it, you know."

"Sure. He's the boss, isn't he? He's right. Who am I to question or challenge him?"

"You are *you*."

"What's that gobbledygook about?" scoffs Paul, though Samuel can see that his questions and patience are starting to calm Paul down.

"Well, last week I learned to remember who I am and how I want to live my life. And I want to pass that along to you. I realize now that I wasn't making good choices. I was letting the company—and Dan—rule my life. Last weekend was my wake-up call, and I had the best time with my family for ages. It put things back in perspective for me."

"And I'm supposed to just do the same, am I? It's not that easy. It's going to take more than one weekend off to improve things for me. I've always wanted to move up in this company, but with Dan in charge, that's just not going to happen. I know I can do it, if he would give me a chance."

"I've heard you say this before," says Samuel. "What's that dream you told me about?"

"That one day I will be running my own company." Paul jumps up and paces impatiently. "But it won't be just any old company. It will be a place where people enjoy coming to work. It will be somewhere they are valued and trusted. Somewhere they can work in the way that suits them. It will be fun, and we'll all work with a passion that our clients can't resist. We will attract all the business we can dream of. We'll be doing something that makes a difference in the world. We won't just be making piles of money for the sake of it. We'll respect each other. We'll listen to and care for each other. Sorry if that sounds soft, but I mean it. I'll be so excited by this company and the people in it that I won't have any problem getting up for work in the mornings."

Samuel smiles. "It's a great picture. Can I come and work with you when you make it happen?"

"As if you'd want to work for me! Maybe Dan will want a job, too." Paul is unable to keep the edge of contempt from his voice. "It's all pie in the sky anyway."

"Is that what you think?" asks Samuel. "I hear such determination in your voice when you talk about it; I wonder why you haven't already made it happen. What's stopping you?"

Paul doesn't notice Samuel glancing at a brightly-coloured card in his hand.

"Well, it's a high-flying idea," says Paul, "and I'm only a backstreet guy made semi-good. I'm not the type of person who rises to great heights."

"Who says?"

"Actually, it's something my mother always says. She's a great lady," Paul says, "but she has no ambitions for herself or for us. She says you have to 'be content with your lot,' make the best of what you have."

"Do you believe that?"

"I try not to. I wouldn't have gone to night school and gained my qualification if I believed it, would I? Yet, whenever I think big, I can't help but hear her voice telling me to be realistic. To stop kidding myself."

"Is that what you believe you are doing?"

Paul takes time to think about this. Samuel's questions are pulling him in. He realizes he has not thought about Dan or the spreadsheets for at least half an hour. He's starting to see that this conversation is about him.

"I believe I've done pretty well up to now. Apart from having Dan as a boss, I thought I had the job I wanted. Now, he's screwing all that up for me. He makes me feel I don't deserve to be here and that my ideas are worthless. I don't think I can take that any more. I've got more to offer. I can't stand that I feel like this."

"What would feel better?" Samuel asked.

"I need to know I have something to contribute; that what I am doing is worthwhile. I want to be listened to. Like you are listening now."

"Have you ever asked Dan what he likes about your work?"

Paul almost choked on his root beer. "Good heavens, no. He doesn't even act like I exist at times. Why would he like my work?"

"How do you know if you don't ask him?"

"But—"

"No, truly," said Samuel, "how do you know if you don't ask him?"

"Well, I'd be pretty scared to ask that. I don't think what he's going to say will be very flattering to me. I don't want to hear it."

"What if he has something good to say?"

"Well, that's what I'd be hoping for," Paul said. "It would build my confidence in myself and what I'm doing here."

"What would it take for you to ask him?"

"A fair bit of courage, which I'm not sure I've got."

"The kind of courage it takes to start a visionary company? The kind of courage it takes to go to night school three times a week after working all day?"

Paul is silent. Deep in thought, he throws the crumbs of his sandwich to the pigeons dipping their wings in the fountains.

Samuel waits. Paul suddenly notices the cards in Samuel's hands. "Here, give me one of those" he says, grabbing randomly at a bright blue card. He looks at it and sighs. His shoulders drop as he realizes what it asks him.

"Okay. You've got me," says Paul at last. "This isn't about Dan at all, is it? It's about me. It's about the stories I tell myself about why I can't do things."

"Possibly," says Samuel. "I don't know for sure. I'm not an expert. But I am coming to realize that there's a lot that goes on inside us that we often blame on things or people around us. That's why I asked you the questions. I'm not sure where I got those questions. They just seemed to come into my head as I listened to you. I'm starting to think that what's going on inside is what determines what we achieve in life. What we decide is important. Does any of this make sense to you?"

"It's starting to," says Paul. "I think it is going to take me some time to unravel what it means. There's a lot in there waiting to be explored. I wonder how often that voice inside my head has stopped me looking at what I want. I need to pay more attention to it."

"If I can help, please let me know," says Samuel. "Maybe we can do more of this learning together."

"I will. Thanks." Paul holds out his hand for Samuel's scrunched up sandwich wrapper and walks to the rubbish bin. "You taking the time today has really helped me. Maybe you could listen and ask me questions more often. Now, let's get back to the hot house."

"Hey, hold on," he shouts after Samuel, who is already striding towards the office building. "You've left those cards. Did you want me to throw them in the rubbish?" Samuel doesn't hear and Paul shrugs his shoulders. Tucking the cards into his jacket pocket to give back later, he has to step to the side to avoid bumping into the woman who suddenly appeared as if through the spray of the fountain. *Did she just whisper something? Was she talking to me?*

May life bring all you wish for, Paul. My name is Tashia.
The phone rings as Paul settles down at his desk again. Dan's extension number comes up on the caller ID. He panics for just a moment, then he takes a deep breath and lets it out slowly as he picks up the receiver with a smile. *No one can make me feel what I don't want to. Neither Mother, nor Dan.*

"Hello, Dan. There's something I'd like to ask you. May I have some of your time this afternoon?"

It would be two years before he looked back on that afternoon and the risky, yet exciting decision he'd made. That afternoon, Paul handed in his notice. It had turned out to be the best moment of his life. That is, if he didn't count the opening of his new factory and the time his team voted him as one of the best employers in the area. As he stood at his office window and admired the extensive city view, he thought, just for a moment, that he caught sight of a vaguely familiar looking woman, looking back at him with a smile.

SIX
Acceptance

Emerging from the fountain with droplets sparkling like a halo in her hair, Tashia turns to Ghoy.

"Another example of the pain caused in this world by those who have gone before," she says. "At least this time he was prepared to listen to what was within him."

"What makes this important for our new community?" asks Ghoy. "How exactly did he change?"

"He stopped resisting his own reality. He came to accept that his inner thoughts are influencing his view of the world. He may not fully understand it yet. I have seen many people search for a long time to understand their inner reality. From this point he can start to understand and learn."

"*Could this be another key to bringing love back into this torn world?*" *asks Ghoy.*

"*Yes, I believe love and acceptance of oneself are important. How can we expect this community to live in peace with one another if each of them cannot first love themselves? Those who went before have had much influence in the messages they passed on to this generation. And yet it is within the power of this generation to replace those messages with what they themselves discover. My hope is that, in doing so, we will leave more helpful messages for those still to come.*"

"*Are you willing to further explore this learning? There may be much we need to understand here,*" *says Ghoy, settling into his customary position by the entrance stone. He pulls his cloak around him against the slight cooling of the evening air.*

"*Of course,*" *says Tashia,* "*It is why I visit the stone circle tonight; to seek your perspective and your wisdom.*"

"*So, what did this young man accept?*" *asks Ghoy.*

"*Acceptance is about letting go of judgment. Judgment of self, judgment of others, judgment of what is right or wrong. True acceptance is trusting that everything is as it is for a reason.*"

"*What gets in the way of such acceptance, for surely it is the easier path?*"

Tashia thinks for a moment. "*It appears this community is reluctant to follow the easier path. Often I see people over-complicate things. This may be a function of thinking—extensive use of the mind at the expense of the heart and the intuition. People judge themselves on what they know or think they know.*

People seem to look for barriers or obstacles in their way. They appear to start from the assumption that things cannot be. Instead of acceptance, they live in denial, particularly a denial of who they are and a denial of self-responsibility.

"It appears that people have been living by unwritten, unspoken rules. They don't question whether those rules serve them well. They delude themselves into believing the rules are the easy path. For many they are. They give up personal freedom and self-acceptance in favour of these rules. To be the same as everyone else. They hide their uniqueness and stay safe.

"Paul is trapped by the rules he carries from his mother, and also by the rules he believes Dan imposes on him. He gives Dan the right to control him. As soon as he acknowledges that this is what is happening, he can move. From the moment he accepts that Dan is impacting him in that way, he reclaims his voice and allows his true self to speak. His unique dream emerges, fuelled by his passion for creating a new company.

"He sees that what is important to him is very different from that imposed on him by others."

"This sounds complicated," Ghoy says.

"I'd like to help more people become aware of and accept their emotions—to help them express their emotions. As soon as an emotion is acknowledged or accepted, we free ourselves from it. Otherwise, emotion gets trapped. It can be buried deep within us because we don't want to acknowledge or accept it. I'd like for people to see that it's not right or wrong to experience emotions. It simply is."

Ghoy nodded. "I recall an ancestor of mine who said that emotions, when not dealt with, can hide in the body and impact us in a physical way, through illness or injury."

"It appears difficult for the community to accept such a concept as yet," says Tashia. "But some believe it to be so."

"At this time, we can encourage the community to be more accepting of themselves, and of others. Acceptance of self is, I believe, one of the most important areas for personal growth. Acceptance of self allows us to free up energy. We witness what is happening and use that energy to move or respond in positive ways. This can impact on what we do and how others experience us. It is time for us to create a community of acceptance."

"Such a community would undoubtedly bring benefit to this land," says Ghoy. "I imagine this will put a stop to fighting wars. The power of acceptance will bring us peace with each other. From there we will grow and regenerate this land. You must continue this work, Tashia. It is too important to ignore."

"Yes," Tashia says, "it is exciting that even one person's acceptance of self can create a positive energy around them, in their relationships and in what they achieve. It frees them up to make choices. On my next journey, I already know that we will explore the community's concept of making choices. I can't wait. Let me leave a reminder of this story before I go."

Tashia moves to the centre of the circle and takes two stones from her pocket. She places a rough nugget of black rock in the circle.

"Let this remind us to look deep into our inner reality and be open to what we might find there.

"This second stone, a piece of pink granite smoothed to the shape of a heart by the winds of years, will remind us of the power of acceptance that starts within each person."

SEVEN

Bryan

Claire throws her car keys on the hall table and kicks off her shoes, dumping a box of homework at the foot of the stairs. A delicious aroma wafts from the kitchen and the song "Wish" by Lighthouse Family is streaming through house speakers.

"Hi," says Paul, appearing in the kitchen doorway with glass of wine for each of them.

"You're home early," Claire grins and kisses him on the cheek. "What's up?"

"I had an interesting chat with Dan today. I'm dying to share it with you. He's pleased with how I am doing my job. I hadn't realized he thought so much of me. I'm just feeling so good about it. I thought I'd get dinner ready and surprise you. What about your day?"

49

"The usual. Lots of fighting in the playground. Not enough time for real conversations with the kids. Teachers complaining about the new regulations for overtime. What are these?" Claire asks, catching the pack of brightly-coloured cards that fall from from a pocket as she hangs Paul's jacket on the hall stand.

"Oh, Samuel had those cards with him today. I think he meant to leave them with me. I was flicking through them this afternoon, just as Dan telephoned me. I said the first question that came into my mind, and it was pretty similar to the words on a bright orange card I was holding at the time. Sounds kind of weird, I know. But anyway, let me tell you about my conversation with Dan..."

The next morning, Claire hears the commotion as soon as she steps out of the car. Waving to Paul as he drives off, she heads for the common room, her arms full of the test papers she marked after dinner last night. She leaves them on one of the sagging old armchairs and heads for the coffee machine.

"You dropped these," says James Murray, a fellow teacher, as he heads out the door with books spilling from the faded canvas bag slung over his shoulder. "Don't worry, I'll go see what that noise is all about.

"I'm sure it's nothing," he adds, somewhat flippantly.

Claire sighs and looks down at her hand, where James has deposited the pack of brightly-coloured cards. *How on earth did they get into my school stuff?* she asks herself, as the bitter, over-roasted coffee hits her veins.

Outside, James' voice rises above the increasingly aggressive shouting of the group in the schoolyard. "That's enough!" he shouts. "You two, see me in my office in ten minutes. The rest of you, break it up and get moving to your next class. The show's over for today." At last he sees the lad cowering on the ground. "Come on, come on. Get up there, Bryan. It's not that bad. You can surely stand up for yourself."

"Yes, sir," mumbles Bryan, the swelling above his eye already throbbing with pain. He pulls his baseball cap down to hide it. By the time he gets to his feet, the teacher is just a shadow to him through the plate-glass door. He picks up his things and heads for the quiet corner of the sports field, where he feels protected by the circle of young elm trees that his class planted three years ago. He sits down on the dry bed of late autumn leaves, turning to catch what he thought was a glimpse of someone in the shadow of the trees.

He's already decided to skip math class again, rather than face those guys who took such pleasure in taunting him. He feels angry and drained of energy. Hopeless. He's determined to stay patient and find his peace again. Some day, he hopes, his tormentors will understand the pain they cause. He wonders, not for the first time, why they are so frustrated and why he is their target.

Claire finds him sitting under the elm trees, as she takes a stroll in the only break her busy timetable allows. "Bryan? What are you doing here? Can I help you with something?" Bryan scrambles to his feet.

"No, no, sit down. Stay there," says Claire, settling herself beside him and pulling her coat tighter against the sharpening wind. "What's this all about?"

She has always been interested in this quiet boy who seems to know his own way through the world. He intrigues her. Maybe this would be her chance to understand him better.

"Were those guys bullying you? What was it all about?" asks Claire gently.

"I never know what it is about," says Bryan. "What I do know is that it's about them, not about me." Claire admires his awareness and encourages him to tell her more.

"When Mr. Murray intervenes, he doesn't actually help," says Bryan. "He gets bossy. Those guys think being bossy is what it's all about. It looks like that's how Mr. Murray got to be where he is today. I wish he would understand why he responds like that. He doesn't care about me or about me being hurt. He just cares about the rules of the school and making sure those don't get broken."

"I'm sure that's not the case," says Claire. "Although I can see how James' reaction might be interpreted in that way."

"What do you think would help?" asks Claire, stuffing her gloved hands into the pockets of her coat, only to find a bright green card there.

"Why do you ask? You're a teacher. Your job is to protect the school too." Bryan's tone is challenging.

"I did not become a teacher to protect school rules at the expense of pupils' learning," says Claire patiently. She knows her profession has suffered from years of strain and conflict with the system. Sometimes she feels like one of the few left with a real sense of purpose around her work. "I love teaching. I love seeing people learn. I love being able to help in problem situations. Maybe like this one. All of that gives me a sense of purpose. I'm not here to serve a system, if that system does not serve the people in it. Do you believe me?"

"Maybe," say Bryan though he doesn't sound convinced, "but how can a system allow this to happen?" He pushes back his baseball cap to reveal the angry purple and yellow bruise on his forehead.

"It's too easy to blame the system," says Claire. "We are all human beings within that system. We have a responsibility towards each other. Perhaps we have forgotten what that responsibility is. Our reasons for doing things, our reactions to situations, and our own responses get muddled up in the pace of our work; in the stress and pressure we are under; in the expectation for us to achieve targets and results. That's what the system judges us by. We don't get any gold stars for taking time for each other or for showing that we care. Ultimately, I still think that's what being a teacher is about; caring enough for others to help them learn and make their way in the world. Of course we can't do everything for them. That would not help in the long run. But what we can do, we *ought* to do while caring for the person. I can't bring myself to see my pupils as statistics in the system, though I suspect some of my colleagues do. It's their way of coping."

"Well, thankfully, there are still teachers like you around," Bryan says, blushing despite himself. "It's strange having this conversation, sitting in a circle of trees with a teacher."

"We are drawn to people with similar intentions in this world," says Claire. "At least that's what my grandmother always said. I'm not sure I understood that before now. Sitting here with you though, we seem to share an understanding. We can choose to be part of that by doing the same as everyone else. Or we can decide that our own sense of purpose is more important, and choose to hang on to it and use that to guide us. I don't mean we'll be perfect. Heaven knows, I've found myself many a time being just as bossy as James, but afterwards I realize that I don't like being like that. I remember that I haven't been caring, even though I believe it to be important, especially with students. It seems to me that you have enough pressures on you—to get good grades, to get a job—that the least I can do is let you know I care for you. I want you to know that not all teachers are thoughtless. For most of us, it's still important that we encourage you to do the best you can, without fear and without judgment. After all, you are our hope for the future. If this world is to get better, I believe we have to help you prepare for that future with a sense of purpose. That, in turn, gives purpose to my days."

"I have always felt a strong sense of purpose," says Bryan. "I try to live with purpose every day."

"That's a very profound statement for a teenager," says Claire. "What does that mean to you?"

"I'm not sure I've tried to explain it before," says Bryan. "It's just inside me. When I get up in the morning, I know that whatever I do that day is important. Everything I say has to come from a positive intention. Like you, my intention is to treat others with caring and respect. I hear a lot of people talk about things like respect, yet I don't think people stop to explore what they mean by respect. James thinks he is being respectful and honourable by stopping a fight. He doesn't consider whether he shows any caring for me. And he tries to get the respect of the bullies through fear and authority. I don't think that is real respect at all. If we are not listening to people, then there is no way we are truly showing them respect. Nor do we deserve their respect.

"I believe that in some strange way, my purpose is to help people remember how to bring true values such as respect and caring back into their lives, their conversations and the way they relate to each other."

Claire smiled. "That sounds like a great subject for your graduation paper, Bryan. I notice you spend more time in social studies class than math class. I'm beginning to understand why. I think you may have some important views to share with people."

"If I choose to do so," says Bryan, getting slightly uncomfortable again. "It's okay sitting here under the trees with you and chatting about it. It doesn't seem silly. I'm not sure my classmates will want to hear it, though."

"Wouldn't this be an example of where you have to choose whether to stay true to your purpose rather than give in to what other people think?" Claire's heart beats loudly at the prospect of Bryan shying away from his convictions again. She doesn't want to push him. She hears the important message behind his words and can imagine the difference it would make if even a few of his peers could listen and take his message to heart.

"Yes," says Bryan, "I see that. Sometimes I get so tired of being the only person to see the world in this way."

"You are not alone," says Claire. "I believe in what you are saying, too. I wish I had seen the world in this way at your age. How may I help you?"

"If, and I'm still saying IF, I choose to explore this in my graduation paper, will you mentor me? Will you help me through the times when I question what I am doing? Will you share your experience and views with me? Will you guide me to things or people who will help me?"

"I'd be honoured," says Claire, her heart bursting with pride and joy at hearing such strong commitment from Bryan. Not everyone has the courage to ask for help. He did not fully believe it himself yet. She couldn't help but be deeply moved by the underlying belief and sense of purpose in what he was saying.

"Here," she says, "I don't know why, but I think it is important that you take these cards. There are questions on them. Use them to remind you of this conversation. Ask yourself the questions, whenever you doubt what you're doing."

Claire hands Bryan the bright green card, along with the other coloured cards that had found their way into her pocket that morning. "You've taught me a lot today, Bryan. Thank you. I remember why I became a teacher. Let's get back to class."

Claire laughs, and reaches up to take the hand pulling her off the crackling bed of leaves. It takes her a moment to realize the strangeness of that hand—Bryan is already halfway across the sports field ahead of her. The rustling leaves all but mask a soft voice that says:

May life be all you claim it to be.

Claire hopes that Bryan has heard it too.

Several weeks later, whistling as he strides into the staff room and deposits his graduation paper in each teacher's cubby hole, Bryan quietly places the coloured cards on top of the pristine white copy in James Murray's box. He allows himself only a small smirk at the thought of James' blood pressure rising as he reads through the unconventional paper, already published on the web and gaining a following among people from all walks of life.

EIGHT
Choice

Ghoy reaches up to remove a dry elm leaf from Tashia's fiery red hair. Together, they enter the stone circle and stop in the shelter of a toppled stone, protected a little from the sharpening wind. The winter sky is soft with deep shrouds of grey clouds, the moonlight streaming out from whichever chink in the cover it can find.

"In Bryan, you have found one of the future generation," says Ghoy.

"Yes, he has chosen a new perspective. This brings him challenges within the existing community. From these, he will learn what is required to bring this new perspective to the attention of others. It will not be easy, but I believe he has the strength required of him."

"What makes him different from the others?" asks Ghoy. "What brought him to your attention?"

"It was how he responded to those who were aggressive towards him," says Tashia. "It is very unusual in the present community for someone to respond to aggression in a peaceful way. I believe him to be a role model for the future."

"Why is he is able to respond so?" asks Ghoy.

"Firstly, he demonstrates high levels of self-awareness. Secondly, he is accepting of the others and their behaviour in a way that enables him to witness it for what it is. He understands that others cannot make him react unless he chooses to do so. He is inquisitive as to why this should be happening around him, and his enquiry will lead him to understand more about others and their behaviours. He takes the time to explore all this, even while the mood of those around him is highly charged and emotional."

"Yet, how can he see that this choice is open to him?" Ghoy is puzzled. "For the most part we witness members of the current community as being very easily triggered by others' behaviours, attitude and language. Why is Bryan so different?"

"He uses the words himself," says Tashia. "He chooses to be patient in the face of others' behaviour. He knows, although he may not fully understand, that his patience will eventually affect their aggression, changing their energy and their response to him."

"How does he make such a choice?"

"That process is not entirely clear to me yet," says Tashia. "I have puzzled over it for some time. I think it is an ability to shift

from the programming of this current society. He seems to follow a different pattern. Bryan asks different questions of himself."

"Are those questions that might help others move into the future?"

"Undoubtedly," says Tashia. "Few people, as yet, demonstrate the ability to use these questions, though some are starting to ask others to help them explore them. I believe that it is only a matter of time until everyone in this community is equipped to ask these questions."

"Perhaps we should include these questions in our guidance to the new communities," says Ghoy, cuing the Scribe to mark the parchment in front of him. "What are these questions to help us make choices for ourselves?"

"I think there are different questions for different levels of choice." Tashia pauses for a moment. "Perhaps you can help me to explore them, so that we may capture them for others."

"Of course," he says.

Tashia is reassured by the knowing wisdom in Ghoy's voice. Once again she feels deeply connected to whatever source they share.

"I believe that first there are choices about how we see and describe ourselves," she says. "The language we use is really important. This has been imprinted on us by those who went before. However, we can find new words, which help us understand ourselves in new ways. This is key to the future. In the old language, we are often critical of ourselves. We assume there is something wrong that needs to be fixed. From this starting point, we are driven to continually prove, correct or improve

61

ourselves. To strive for some imaginary concept of perfection that doesn't even exist. As we do so, we miss out on the beauty of ourselves and our immediate surroundings.

"The choice I wish for the community of the future is that each of us may use new words of self-appreciation. We will give up such words as 'try' and 'should'; 'ought to' and 'must.' We will stop feeling like victims, conditioned by fear. We will recognize our truth more clearly.

"We will confidently declare our wants, our needs. We will use words like 'I can,' and 'I will.' Our language will give us courage, trust and belief in ourselves. We will move on from our judgements and criticisms. We will make our own choices and be with each other in new conversations. It will be a language of love.

"We will learn to slow down, to step outside ourselves in the moment and ask four key questions:

'What am I aware of?'

'How might I usually respond?'

'How would I prefer to respond to this situation or person?'

'What response do I now choose?'

"This will not come easily to us. We will need conscious practice. In doing so, we will learn to know ourselves better. We will recognize the patterns we have adopted in our responses to people and to situations. Then we will choose new ways to respond. Only then will we understand how to make choices that serve us better."

Ghoy interjects at this point. "Using the current language of the community, I fear that making choices for ourselves may be seen as selfish."

"Yes. There is a new, and yet at the same time ancient, wisdom to this process of self-choice. It has been forgotten by the current community. It is one of the reasons for their current troubles. For them, the concept of self and therefore self-choice has come to mean separate from others. This idea creates barriers between self and others, which become insurmountable. This separation has been exacerbated by many of the technologies they introduced; technologies that eliminated the need for close communities; technologies that enabled individuals to hide from each other and never meet face to face. People have become lost. They have neglected their own needs for connection and conversation."

"Many would continue to see this as good," says Ghoy.

"Perhaps. Sometimes it is simply a way to be comfortable that what we are doing meets the expectations of our current community. Our programming again. The choice, I am suggesting here, is to change that programming and see oneself with new eyes."

"Go on," says Ghoy, intrigued by this topic.

"When we first came to this community, we were taught that we are all one; that we are all connected. We have sought to bring our spiritual, scientific and technological understanding to this question. On many levels it can be demonstrated to be so. And yet we doggedly resist believing it to be so. When this community comes to recognize this again, we will see that the

only element of community for which we are responsible and accountable is self. We will learn again that what we choose for self, impacts those around us. We will remember that, if we change ourselves, we help change everything and everyone we come into contact with."

"Can you enlighten us further, perhaps with examples from those in the community you have just visited?" asks Ghoy.

"Yes, I can," says Tashia. "Bryan exercises self-choice. He chooses patience as a response to aggression. He chooses understanding rather than judgement. He chooses courage rather than fear. As a result of these choices, he impacts positively on Claire. Although, by conventional standards, she is the teacher and he the pupil, his perspective reminds Claire of her deeper sense of purpose and reignites the passion she feels for the true nature of her work.

James, by contrast, shows a lack of self-choice. He responds automatically to the situation in the playground. He wades in heavy-handed, with no thought as to the consequences. A lesser soul than Bryan would have felt let down and abandoned by his approach. A lesser soul than Bryan would not have recognized that James' behaviours could be seen to justify the bullies' behaviours. James missed an opportunity to have a positive impact on everyone involved."

"How might he have done that?"

"By slowing down to ask himself the four key questions, and by considering whether his response would have a short-term or long-term impact. With awareness, he might have addressed the real issue: why the bullies behave as they do. As yet, James is not practiced enough to help others find real causes and solutions. This will take time for James, as it will for others in the community. We can guide them."

"You suggested that there are several layers of self-questions," says Ghoy. "What other questions do the members of the future community need to ask?"

"This world is about choice. Our true success lies in recognizing and living by the choices we make. Those choices are neither right nor wrong. We will meet many people who make different choices from us. This creates a rich patchwork of learning. We may learn from our own choices. We may learn from the choices of others. We may change our own choices as we learn from each other.

"There are powerful questions to be recorded here." At his point Tashia looks up to check that the Scribe is still writing, and then continues.

"'How do I know and define my true self?'

'What pulls me away from my true self?'

'When that happens, what do I need to bring me back to my true self?'

"These are examples of healthy self-choices," says Tashia, "and of people who have the courage to live by them. On my journeys I have also suggested people ask:

'What, in my life, will I not compromise or neglect, no matter what tries to pull me away from it?'

"It seems to me that, by being aware of our true self-choice, we gain a freedom with it. We can trust it. Our choices release us from fear and compromise."

65

As the flat light of day begins to touch the stones, Tashia stands and stretches. Again she has gathered two stones on her journey. She places a warm amber gem down in the circle.

"This amber reminds us to look for the richness of our deepest intentions and sense of purpose," she says. "This second, a smooth round opalescent white pebble, signifies the purity of choice, which can be ours, if only we wish to make it so."

Together Ghoy and Tashia descend the grassy slope from the stone circle as an early skylark flits to join the migrating flock.

"With such choices, we too can fly."

NINE
James

Across the car park, James watches Claire scrape the frost from the windscreen of Paul's car before getting into the passenger seat. He wishes he could feel the way she does about teaching. But he doesn't. He can't pretend any more. He suspects the students know how he feels. Sometimes they tease and torment him. His lack of interest makes him an easy target. He wonders how he got to this point. He feels so tired. So stuck. At one time teaching was his whole life, but now it's just not as fulfilling as it once was. Something has changed.

As he turns into the street on his bicycle, he is thrown to the dark icy ground. The sound of the screeching tires and breaking glass clashes with the intense pain shooting up his left hip. He hears vague screams as a heavy blackness descends on him.

"Wake up, James," a soft voice says, shaking him gently. "You'll be all right. We've given you some medication for the pain, and you will feel drowsy for a while. Take a sip of water."

James blinks in the harsh light of the hospital ward as a young nurse helps him to sit up and drink from the glass she holds to his lips. He takes in only the empty bed to his right, the smell of antiseptic and the curtains closed in front of him, before he drifts off again.

It is morning when he wakes up again. The bruised muscles up his side ache as he tries to stretch. He is hungry, and yet is aware that there are more important things to focus on. He has been so distracted recently. Something like this was bound to happen.

No answers come to him before the doctor appears on her rounds. Mary, as it says on her name badge, tells him that, luckily, there is no permanent damage. He has a slight concussion and some severely torn ligaments. It could have been a lot worse. James nods obediently as she berates him for not paying more attention to the traffic.

Perhaps this was a wake-up call. There is more than traffic to pay attention to in his life at the moment; things that have been troubling him for months now. *Six weeks at home with his feet up? That's just he what he needs. Enforced thinking time. No escape.*

Three days later, the doorbell rings, and he hobbles over to open it. Claire holds out a bunch of supermarket flowers and a huge bag of his favourite peppermint creams. *How could she know that?*

"Hi there," she greets him cheerily. "I never know whether people like flowers or not, but they do brighten the place up a bit." She looks around the room and pulls open the curtains, revealing a heavy morning frost on the windows.

"Looks like you've been letting things go a bit around here," she says, with more than a hint of intrigue in her voice. "What's up with you?"

James welcomes her question. It opens the floodgates to everything he's been thinking about for the past few days. "Do you really want to know?" he asks, throwing another log on the roaring winter fire. The flames dance against the blackened brickwork of the chimney, encircling them and casting an unusually human-like third shadow across the wallpaper.

"Sure," says Claire, "that's what I came for. I suspect there's more than a torn ligament bothering you. I've seen it coming for a while. What have you been ignoring?" She pours two cups of coffee from the percolator. "So come on, spill the beans. I'm listening."

James wonders how long it has been since he felt listened to. There hasn't been anyone around to listen to him for some time—not since Samantha moved out; not since he gave up Friday nights at the pub with Tim and Daniel; not since he last went on holiday with his cousin Frank. He realizes he's been hiding away. That's not like him.

"My life feels like it is changing. I don't know what's happening. I don't enjoy my job anymore. I don't want to spend

69

time with friends, doing the things we've enjoyed doing for years. I can't be bothered with the garden. Something is changing, but I don't know what it is or why."

"Go on," says Claire. "I'm listening. Maybe you need to talk it out to understand it."

"Yes, maybe," he says. "I've certainly been thinking a lot since my bike accident. It's kind of scary."

"What's scary about it?" asks Claire.

"What's scary is the mix of things going on inside me. Sometimes I hate what I'm doing. I lose my patience with the kids at school. I don't get excited any more to see them learning. I don't care. Then I get guilty about not caring. Then I try too hard to convince them I care. Then I just end up not knowing what I'm doing or saying. They think I'm a hopeless teacher. Especially those guys who bully the likes of Bryan. They think they can get the better of me, too. I'm fed up with it all. I don't want to do it any more."

"That's a pretty strong statement," she says. "Are you sure? What would you rather do?"

"Well, that's the funny thing. I feel awful about how things are going at school, like I don't want to be there any more. But I have a strange excitement going on inside me too. The only thing that helps me is to come home and play the saxophone. The music helps me."

"What is it about the music that helps you?" asks Claire. She has heard him play both the sax and the piano at school concerts, and in the pub down the road. She knows he is good.

"When I play music, I feel alive. I feel that's what life is about. I feel as though nothing else matters. I want everyone around me to be part of it too. How corny does that sound? More and more, playing music is all I want to do. I've been thinking that maybe that's what I want to do with my life. Play music. Maybe help others to play music."

"That would be a big change," says Claire. "Are you going to do it?"

"How can I? What would people think? 'Professional teacher turns into musical drop-out.' Explain that to everyone."

"What's going to happen if you don't make the change?" asks Claire, holding her hands towards the dancing flames in the fireplace.

"Who cares? I'll just carry on. Take the salary. Get the pension. At least it's safe." James shrugs as he drains his coffee cup.

"What's stopping you, then?"

"I just told you. The job. The security. The pension. Not things to give up lightly, no matter how much I want to play music."

"What's stopping you?"

"I told y—"

"No, don't give me the same old answers again," says Claire. "I've heard you play. I've always thought you could be a professional musician. What's stopping you?"

James resists the temptation to repeat himself again. He can hear himself rolling out those excuses. Then, he hears another voice inside himself. It's coming from his heart. It's a quiet, shaky voice. It's a scared voice. Somehow, he feels Claire can hear it too.

"I'm scared," he laughs nervously. "I'm just too scared to make such a change at my stage in life. I'd be throwing away everything I've done so far. And for what? Some aimless career in the fickle world of music. How sensible is that?"

"Does it have to be sensible to make you happy?" asks Claire. "Maybe more of us need to make a change in our life to be happy. I remember what life was like before I was made 'redundant' from the software house. I hated it. The change was scary, as you say, but I've never looked back. It turned out for the best."

"Well, that's different. Your change was forced on you. That's an easy option."

"I don't think so," says Claire stiffly. "I still had to make some choices about how to turn my life around. It took a lot of guts and more than a few nights of tears to retrain as a teacher. At least you are making your own choice, if you choose to."

"It still feels like a huge cliff. I don't know if I want to climb it or if I'll fall off it and end up more bruised and battered than I am now."

"There's no way of knowing that, either, is there?" says Claire. "There are only two options: either you hide from the change, deny it and continue to live unhappily. Or you can go for it, open your arms to the possibilities it offers you and see what happens. The very least that can come of it is that you learn something."

"Too late by then if I've got no roof left over my head," says James, determined to be cynical.

"It's your choice," says Claire getting up to leave. "You may only get this one chance. Face the fear, as they say, and do it.

"I used to think it was easy to say that, but you know I think it is hard sometimes to do what it takes. Decide to do it, admit what you are scared of, find someone to help and support you and off you go. Can't be any worse than what's happening now, can it?"

She turns to heads out the door. "And by the way, how secure is that pension if you're not enjoying your work anymore? You better watch out the school board doesn't spot that you've stopped teaching with enthusiasm."

James throws the cushion from the sofa at the door as it closes. "Thanks for the vote of confidence," he shouts, but he can't help laughing. Claire has this way of making things seem more positive. She always looks on the upside of things. She can always see the possibilities. Maybe that's what helps her face change head on.

He hobbles to the shower. As the hot water hits his sore shoulders and back, James finds himself singing. The song reminds him to follow his dreams and not be one of the crowd.

What would it take? he muses, as he towels himself dry. He feels more positive than he has for ages. He grabs the telephone and taps out Tim's number.

"Hey Tim, got time for a pint?" He almost yells into the phone as he struggles into his Levis. "I want to resurrect that idea for the music school we talked about last year. I have

73

a feeling the time is ripe for it now. Yeah, meet you there in forty minutes."

He's already working out how many students he'll be able to inspire to follow careers in music. He lays the phone down again on a pile of old newspapers; on the table are some brightly-coloured cards and Bryan's well-thumbed paper—a paper he's read about twenty times in the last few days.

A tune he's never heard before pops into his head, the gentle refrain of a soft feminine voice: *May life be all you claim it to be.*

TEN
Reflection

Tashia shivers as she emerges from the fire Ghoy has lit in the centre of the circle. A dusting of snow settles on the stones. He smiles when he sees her.

"It appears that your journey, this time, has led to a significant change for James. To make such a significant choice and start his life off in a new direction is no small step. Perhaps this is what more of the new community needs to do. What will it take, do you think?"

Tashia sits silently before responding. "I feel that people need to understand more of the nature of change and their own ways of dealing with it, whether that is change on a larger scale such as James is exploring, or whether it is a small change they wish to make. In either case, I have found it important that people stop to reflect before they embark on any change.

"It appears that people often feel that change is outside their own control. That change is something imposed on them. This saddens me, for it means they don't fully use their capacity to create change and may not take full responsibility and account-ability for their own life. I have seen great capacity, within the people chosen for the future, to not only respond positively to change, but to actively embrace and create changes for the better in their lives. I don't believe we came here to live a life unfulfilled. I believe we came to be happy.

"People seem to hear threat and fear at the prospect of change, to perceive that change is bad. We need to reflect more powerfully on the potential good that comes from change. That potential good is not often immediately obvious to us. We have to first develop the capability to ask a new question, to see some-thing from another perspective, before we can actively look for the good in how we might change it."

"This appears to be another complex issue," says Ghoy. "Have you discovered any ways to make it clearer to the people of the future community? What can we teach about change?"

"As I see it, the key lies in slowing down for reflection. True reflection helps us to realize what is happening to us and how we are responding to it. True reflection is where we challenge ourselves to ask what we need to learn to move forward. True reflection helps us uncover the fears that lie within us and which, so often, stop us from making positive changes in our thoughts, our feelings and our behaviours, and from seeing new possibilities for our lives.

"I have tried, for many of my journeys now, to understand how people are fearful. Yet, fear is often just a story in our mind. It may not be real. If each person reflects on that fact alone, I am convinced it will lead them down paths they might not otherwise have explored. Apart from real crises, most fear is imaginary. It is the product of what we create in our mind's eye, influenced by our past experience and conditioning. It prevents us digging deep within for the courage to take a new step; to go to the cliff, as James put it, look over the edge, see what is there and then to make a choice on whether to risk stepping over it.

"I'm not saying people have to go blindly into the future. Often there is no way of knowing for sure what any given change will bring. We don't know that it will be good, but we don't know that it will be bad, either. And who are we to judge things as good or bad, anyway? Everything is brought to us as part of our learning and our preparation for the new community. Until we try it out, until we are prepared to learn from it and, most importantly, take the time to reflect on what we are experiencing from it, then this community will be perpetually bound by its current limitations. I despair of this being so."

"How then," he asked, "do we encourage people to reflect more? Shall reflection time be a pillar for the future community?"

"That would be wonderful, if we were to truly value reflection time and ask ourselves the questions we do not otherwise ask. If taking such reflection time were deemed to be essential to our health, and to our capacity to fulfill our lives. Sadly, this has been lost in the busyness of the most recent community. It is reappearing in some places. Those who crave reflection time are making more time for it. Yes, I think we should confirm with the Future Guides that reflection time is crucial to the foundation of the new community. Only in reflection time, will people come to remember the questions that truly help them. Only in reflection will they feel able to ask for help and guidance along the way. Only in reflection time will they start to capture the learning that will guide a different path to the future.

"Reflection is about playing things back, looking at each scene and what it meant—not to over-analyze and certainly not to lose ourselves in what went wrong, but rather to seek the learning and key messages that will build a better pathway for ourselves the next time we find ourselves in a similar situation."

"What form would this reflection time take?" asks Ghoy.

"There are many ways to enjoy fruitful reflection: walking in nature, swimming in clear water, relaxing with friends, listening to someone else's story, taking the time to ask meaningful questions, disciplining oneself to attend regular exercise or yoga classes, learning to meditate, taking time to breathe, or listening to your own body. All of these offer us the opportunity to hear, learn and remember parts of ourselves that we have forgotten. This is where we will overcome our imaginary fears and find the courage to make major and minor changes, however large or frightening they first appear. I wish it so for our future community."

"Yes, these are truly valuable words of guidance. I, too, wish it so."

Tashia lays a clear crystal by the edge of the fire, its light refracting outwards from the glory of the flames. "This crystal brings us clarity for reflection and its many angles remind us of the many choices that are open to us to change things for the better. All we have to do is take the time to look for them.

"I am also leaving a handful of sand to signify the potential for change which lies within us. This sand was once solid stone, which has transformed over time. And it will change again, in due course, to be but small grains of interference. Let it remind us to keep a clear perspective on change and face it with courage and trust."

The moon rises to join their reflection on the ice as Ghoy and Tashia pull their thick woollen cloaks around themselves to keep out the bite of winter, settling by the fire to await the next journey.

ELEVEN
Mary

James grimaces, as he straightens his leg.

"That's it," says Mary. "That's good. Your muscle is almost back to full strength. This is your final check-up. I don't need to see you again. Congratulations. You must be looking forward to getting back to the classroom."

"Actually, Doctor, I'm not going back." James can't help grinning as he gets up, and hands Mary a copy of the brochure for his music school before leaving the treatment room. "I'm just off to take a look at a potential studio with my friend, Tim. Goodbye and thanks for everything."

Mary looks at his back in amazement as the doors swing closed behind him. *How wonderful*, she thinks, *to have the courage to do what you want to do with your life*. Her appointment book confirms that James is her last patient today, and so she grabs her coat, stuffs the brochure into her bag to look at later and heads to the elevator, already thinking of her shopping list for the supermarket. Catherine and Mark, her children, are coming for Friday night supper, a habit they have enthusiastically maintained ever since they left home for their own apartments. Mary welcomes the warm spring breeze after the stuffy atmosphere of the hospital and decides that a light salad will be in order for supper. *We can sit in the garden.* The circular lawn bordered by budding daffodils is her favourite spot at this time of year.

Catherine and Mark arrive within ten minutes of each other. *Both inherited their father's punctuality*, thinks Mary as she welcomes them with a glass of homemade elderberry wine that was surprisingly good last season. "Mark, help me with these last two dishes, and we can get settled in the garden. We'll just catch the last of the sun." The soft rays of sunshine filter across the daffodil beds, as an extra large lily head, almost human, bows down, listening.

"How has your week been?" Her usual question comes as no surprise to either of her grown-up children. It's her weekly reassurance that all is well in their worlds.

"Well—" starts Catherine at the same time as Mark throws up his hands with a groan of despair. "Ooops," she says, "I guess you need to go first then." She is already anxious to know what is troubling her younger brother.

"It looks like there will be more job cuts at the bank," says Mark. "It's frustrating people now. I don't know how much longer till my name appears on the list. They are saying nobody is safe, now that the merger with our overseas partner is going ahead."

"But Mark, you've done so well there, surely your job is safe?" Her tone is half statement and half question. "You've always enjoyed your work there."

"I don't think that is any guarantee for the future, though." Mark shrugs his shoulders and pushes a few salad leaves around his plate. "I'm thinking it might be time for a new career. I can't imagine what I might do, though."

"And what about your week, Catherine?' asks Mary. "Do you have some good news? What's happening with your research project?"

"It's going very well, actually," says Catherine, still looking with concern at her brother. "We got next year's budget approved, and that means we can go ahead and hire another research assistant. That will bring the project forward by about six months. I see huge opportunities in the marketplace for the new component, and I'm working on a proposal for the company to break into a whole new business stream as a result. There are some challenges with that, of course. Not everyone can see the possibilities. Sometimes I wonder if it would not be easier to get out there and do it myself—start the new business stream, I mean."

Mary sits for a moment, enjoying the last of her wine. Mark has gone to make coffee, and she can smell the fresh aroma as he grinds the beans she picked up an hour ago. The sun is deep on the horizon, and the birds are starting to gather for the evening. The daffodils around her are closing for the day. As she savours this moment, an image of James running out of the therapy room earlier that day comes back to her. She remembers the grin on his face and the youthful energy that surrounded him. She remembers again that he had made a huge change in his life. She feels a sense of impatience with herself and, if she is honest, with her two grown-up children. A question comes to mind as Mark returns with the coffee.

"Tell me, both of you—" Mark and Catherine both look up "—what would you be doing now, if you could wave a magic wand and do anything you want to? What is it that you want to do, be, have, and experience in your life, if anything were possible?"

"Wow, that's some question," says Mark, a list starting to form in his mind. "There is a lot on my list."

"Mine too," says Catherine. "You go first."

"Well, where will I start?" says Mark. "Okay, here goes: I've been cooped up in that bank since I was seventeen. I want to go on some adventures. I want to know more of the world, how people live in different cultures. I want enough money to have a sense of freedom and to be able to make my own choices. I'd like a nice car. I can see myself running a marathon. I want to white-water raft somewhere like the Grand Canyon. I want to know how to cook apple pie and to always have time for conversations like this. I want to find someone special to share my life with. I want to take photos of those people I meet around the world. I want to tell their stories, so that people can learn from each other. I want to show that this world is not all about banks and about money. And I'd like to have a dog again."

"That's quite a list," says his mother proudly. "With all those ideas, how come you are still at the bank, anyway? What about you, Catherine?"

"Gosh, I think my list sounds a bit serious compared to Mark's. I've been thinking while he was speaking, and I get excited at the possibility of taking the new product to the market myself. I've always had a yearning to lead a team. I think I'd like to set up a company to do that. Wow! Where did that come from? What else do I want to do, have, be and experience in life? There are a few more things. Like building a medical clinic in Africa to spend part of each year doing volunteer work there. To write a book about the experience and sell the book to make more money for the clinic. To always come back here for suppers with my family. And when I've got time, I want to do a parachute jump." She reaches over to touch her mother's hand as Mary cringes at this thought. "What else? I want to have tea with Bono, take singing lessons, join a drama group. But most of all I just want to be happy."

The three of them sit in the silent excitement of the moment, imagining all the possibilities they have just painted. Pictures ambitiously different, stretching a long way into the distance from what they both do at the moment. In the silence, Mary reaches for a tissue from her handbag, and instead finds James' music school brochure. As she pulls it out, she watches a number of coloured cards fall out and land randomly on the grass at her feet.

85

"What about you, Mum? You don't get off without answering the question too," laughs Catherine.

"Well, apart from seeing you both live your dreams—with the exception of parachute jumps, maybe—there are some things I'd still like to do as well. I don't think my life is over yet. I remember your Great Aunt Lena's trick of staying young by not telling her body how old it really was."

"Yes, you're just coming into your own." Catherine laughs along with her mother, as they start to clear the supper dishes into the kitchen. "So what do you want?"

"You know, I've been thinking about that since a patient left my office today. He is making a complete change in his career. I don't think I want to change my career. I enjoy medicine, and I enjoy being able to do it part-time. Yet I want to stretch my mind again. There are so many new things to learn. I could imagine studying a few days a week to get a specialist degree. Then I could come help in your clinic. Apart from that, there are a couple of things on my 'always wanted to do list.' Meeting Oprah is one of them, *as if.*" She laughs at the thought. "Swimming with dolphins is another, then there's living for a whole month on a remote Scottish island, having a weekend in Paris, and figuring out the new computer system at work. Lots of things. They are just dreams."

"I wonder," says Catherine, "What turns these dreams into reality? What if these are the things we are supposed to be doing in our lives? What if that's where our true potential lies? Not in the routine of the jobs we currently have? What would it take for us to follow just one of those dreams?"

"Now I don't know if I ought to have started this conversation," says Mary, as she stacks the dishwasher.

"No, don't worry about that. Surely this is exactly the type of conversation that leads people to expand their horizons. I'm feeling energized by the ideas we've shared. I've had the idea of starting the company for some time now. I was scared to admit it to myself. Now that I've spoken it out loud, and now that you've heard it and haven't laughed at me, it feels like something that could happen. I'm excited about it."

"Whoa, there," says Mark, caught up in the energy of his sister's idea. "Things are starting to move a bit fast around here, aren't they? We were only talking about things we might want?"

"Yes, what if you were out there taking photos and spreading stories of people's way of life around the world? You were always great at stories, Mark. People will want to listen to you. Maybe that's what you need to be doing. Maybe the bank will pay you off and you'll be able to go and do it. Promise me you will."

"I'm not ready to promise anything," says Mark, feeling a strong pull to the photograph albums that lie on the bookshelf by the kitchen window; the pictures he took on last year's trip to Australia and New Zealand. There was so much about the aboriginal way of life that offered up stories. Maybe there was a book there already.

"So, what one step might we each take, in the next three months, to move towards one of these future dreams? Where would you start?" asks Mary, gently pushing them all towards action.

"Well, I'm going to phone Jeff Johnson tomorrow morning," says Catherine. "He's an investor I met at last week's product launch. I chatted with him about my ideas for the new component. I think he might be a good starting point if I want to explore a business plan and get investment for it. *And* I'm going to go ahead and book that trip to Africa. Want to come with me, Mum?"

Mary is quietly amazed at the size of Catherine's first step. Typical of her go-ahead nature. "Yes," she says, "I would like that very much. Let's explore some dates."

"Well, I'm not going to let you speed off with your ambitions and leave me in the dust," laughs Mark. "I think I'll start more slowly though. No point losing out on a package, if the bank is going to pay me off. I'm going to get started on these albums from last year. With the notes I made in my diary, I think there might already be a good story there. My aim will be to get an article published within the next year, maybe in a travel journal. Who knows?"

Mary can't help but admire their thinking. All she had done was ask simple, yet powerful, questions, which had uncovered a wealth of hopes and dreams in both her children. They had revealed possibilities she never suspected they were holding. Imagine if she had never heard their dreams? She had thought working in their respective careers was what success was about. She'd been proud to share their achievements and promotions as they both climbed the career ladder. Now she realizes that their jobs represent only part of them. *They have big hopes for the future, and they both show a sense of responsibility for people and for this world.*

And all it had taken were some questions, she thinks as she puts fresh water in the vase of daffodils on the kitchen windowsill and tidies away the brochure, coloured cards and other mail she had laid on the countertop.

TWELVE
Renewal

Tashia stretches her arms to embrace the dampness in the spring air. Like a sunlit spring bud, thought Ghoy, smiling quietly again and waiting for her latest insights to surface. Tashia has been the right choice. She fulfills her purpose well. The Future Guides are proud of her progress. The new community is emerging.

"Spring once again brings us new perspectives," says Tashia as she lets a stream of tiny, multicoloured and vibrant crystals trickle through her fingers to scatter amongst the stones gathered in her previous journeys. "This is, I believe, the most joyful part of all my journeys. To see the birth of a new idea, a new perspective, a new response, a new pathway—all contributing to a new way of life. All the individual ways in which the people

of my journeys are experiencing a sense of renewal combine to create the shift towards our desired future. I imagine all those people, their thoughts and ideas, converging, like some unseen web of creation—above, around and to the heart of the new community. I imagine the power of each of those moments of renewal, sending their light outwards with the myriad energy of all the others, to jostle the eyelids and the lips of those yet to open to renewal."

"It is indeed a joyous thought," says Ghoy. "And one which serves our intention well. It was for such vision that you were chosen for this work. Your sense of creation intermingles with those coloured crystals, like the oxygen that once sustained clean and healthy life prior to the destruction. May it continue to do so."

"As I see each person from my journeys going on their way, I wonder how much longer it will need to be so. How many more journeys are needed before there is enough energy for our future dream to be realized?" asks Tashia. "For while there is much reward to be found in this work, I sense an emerging need for my own renewal. It is but a tiny spark within me, and I need to attend to it."

"You have learned well, Tashia," says Ghoy. "It is, indeed, vital that you take care of yourself. The Future Guides expect you to do so. Your current journey may indeed be drawing to a close, however, there will be more work—perhaps in another time—for you to complete. Such loving care and intuition as yours will continue to serve well. You are right to attend to yourself. What is it you need at this time?"

"*My needs are simple. I have learned to live well, perhaps better, now that I have let go of many of the attachments of the old ways. I need little more than the freedom to be myself, to relax, reflect and honour the learning that I have discovered on these last journeys. This is all I need.*"

"*How will you fulfill this need for yourself?*" asks Ghoy.

Tashia knows he asks this with no attachment, assumption or expectation that he has the right to satisfy these needs in her. Rather, his questions serve to further her reflection on how to truly find the renewal she seeks at this time. Tashia cannot help but remind herself how rare such leadership is, even among the Future Guides. Ghoy alone combines the strength and humility to serve, in a way few others do. May that one day, someone, somewhere, even once, will think of her in the same way.

This thought brings her back to focus on the question again. "*What do I need?*

"*When I am satisfied that the key messages from my journeys can be shared throughout the new community; when I know that those who need them have access to those insights; then I will retreat to the energy of the mountains and let the fresh air cleanse my mind, my heart and my soul. Then I, too, will feel honoured by this world of renewal.*"

"*So what will help you claim this for yourself?*"

Tashia hears the words even before Ghoy expresses them, and the picture she has been waiting for flashes into her mind, projected in a clear silver light in front of her eyes and then settling into the deep resonating beat of her heart.

"It is in the circle," she says, spinning around with her arms outstretched. "These stones have witnessed the story of each journey. They in turn now carry the awareness, the sense of acceptance, the choices, the reflections and the vital energy of renewal, which all those who follow will need. It remains for me only to seal that learning within this circle, to be shared as a power with all circles to come. From this point on, may those circles bring guidance to the peoples."

Ghoy waits, listening with all his senses, to her joy.

"Will you help me?" she asks, as she comes to stillness, aware as she slows that the energy continues to spin around her, upward and outward in turquoise, orange and cream shards, creating fire across the northern sky.

"I am honoured to do so," whispers Ghoy, for he knows she already had her own answer.

"May the future be all you dream it to be, Tashia."

THIRTEEN
Dan

Dan tries surreptitiously to ease the tightness of his collar, hoping the TV camera is focusing on the interviewer and not on him at that moment. He wants to wipe the sweat from his brow and hopes instead that the unsavoury makeup experience he endured before coming on stage is doing its job. He focuses on the interviewer's question, still not entirely comfortable to be here. He can't believe they couldn't find someone better to give the Entrepreneur of the Year award to.

"So, Dan, with this award, IF-Q Corporation is being held up as a shining example to up-and-coming businesses. What message do you want to pass on to the entrepreneurs and leaders of the future?" The interviewer pins him with a plastic smile.

"Well," says Dan, and he knows he is about to tell a long story. It's so much what he wants the leaders of the future to hear, and he's soon talking with real passion. He can see the interviewer relax back into her chair, mesmerized by his words and fascinated by the message behind them. It feels like the whole world is listening to him.

"For twenty years I headed up IF-Q Corporation and, I confess, didn't do that great a job for most of those years. I realize that now. Not as far as the people in the company were concerned. However, I gave it my best shot. I had come up through the ranks and, to be honest, didn't know any better. It had been drilled into me that business was about profit, so I figured all I had to do was put profit before everything else, and we'd do well.

'Now I'm beginning to rethink all that. It takes some courage for me to sit here and say this in front of goodness knows how many people watching this interview. But hang it all, I'm coming to the end of my career. Sure, I can still influence a lot, but mainly I want to get out of the way and make sure that the new leaders of the IF-Q Corporation will do things differently.

"I've come to believe that the most important reason for having a business—any business where people are going to spend a significant part of their life—is for that business to be a place where people have a sense of purpose, a sense of belonging, a sense of community. I never thought I'd hear myself using this type of woo-woo language, but as you can tell, I've become mighty convinced about this. IF-Q

Corporation now has almost half a million employees. That's a hell of a lot of unhappiness in the world if those employees are not getting what they need from their work. That's also a lot of potential and energy, which, if it's not channelled in the right way, is being wasted. Think what might be possible if we harness that energy and inspire people. We go on all the time about wanting people to be creative and innovative; if that's what we want for the future, then there's a lot that needs to change in our businesses to make that possible.

"I've come to see that it's not only about profit. In the long run, it's about making sure people have what they need to live fulfilled lives. Successful business is a by-product of enthusiastic, inspired people, and I'm proving that to be right. I've learned to become a different person from that 'profit only' leader. People around me have changed. In fact, we make more money now than we used to. I'm not quite sure how that happens, but I'm convinced it has something to do with clients wanting more of what we offer because they enjoy their contact with our people so much."

"Surely, it's easy to say all these good words," interjects the interviewer with no small amount of skill. "What does it take to make it happen?"

"Yes," says Dan. "You're right. I had to take a really good look at myself and the world around me. It was a scary thing to do. Scarier than the toughest business deals I've handled. When I got over the scary bit, I felt better about a whole lot of things.

"First, I learned that people are forever changing. Each person is an individual going through different phases of their lives. We don't all go through the same phases at the same time, so when you have a group of people working together—a team—there can be so much going on. As a leader I've learned to listen and trust that whatever is happening is okay. Old Mr. Fix-It in me always wanted to have the answer for everyone. Now I think I play a better role just by being there, creating the right environment for people while they follow their own path, troubled as that may sometimes be for them."

"I don't want to stop your flow, Dan; I can see you are passionate about your people, so I would like you to give us some more concrete advice or guidance on how exactly you take this new, enlightened approach." The interviewer sits forward on the edge of her leather chair.

"I can sum it up in five steps," says Dan eagerly. "Hopefully I can make them clear, but please stop me and ask if anything doesn't seem to make sense."

"I'll be glad to," says the interviewer with a smile—her producer calls 5 minutes in her earpiece. "Please go on."

"Thanks. Here are the five things I remember: it's about being **aware** of myself in every situation or conversation; it's about **accepting** that others see things from different perspectives and that all those perspectives have value so I don't waste time judging or criticizing them—rather I listen to find the value in their perspective. It's about remembering there is always a **choice**, always another way beyond what we might always have done or haven't yet thought about doing. It's about slowing down to **reflect** on why, how and whether things are working well. And it's about taking care of myself and people around me so that we always have the opportunity to be **renewed**, energized and refreshed so that we can sustain our success.

"It's funny," says Dan, and the interviewer clasps more tightly at her notepad, fearing he is about to go off track. "Sometimes, all I've done in a conversation is listen, totally focused on the other person. Sometimes I haven't had to say very much, if anything at all. At other times, I've noticed the most powerful, yet sometimes simplest, questions occur to me, and when I ask them, it's like a light bulb goes on and the other person finds the answer they have been looking for. I still can't work out how or why that happens.

"Anyway, where was I? I could talk about this stuff all day if you want me to. Let me tell you some stories…"

Dan sits smugly back into the studio sofa as the interviewer casts an appealing eye towards the director's window. Just then she hears the director's voice in her earpiece saying, *Ladies and gentlemen, we've just been advised that due to atmospheric interference with the satellite our next program has been delayed. Our current interview with Dan, the retired executive of IF-Q Corporation, is therefore being extended.* The interviewer turns back to Dan.

"So are you saying that the role of a new-style leader is to help people recognize and use these five steps in their daily life and work?" She is conscious of the need to move Dan on.

"Yes, I guess I am," says Dan with a smile that belies his age and reveals a twinkle of energy that suggests he can still inspire those following him. "That's exactly what I am saying. Let me tell you just a few stories that will demonstrate how life changed for people I know. I think it was the changes in other people that opened my eyes to new possibilities.

"Firstly, there was Samuel. He works for me in the contracting department. He realized that putting all his energy into work was destroying his personal life. When he became aware of that, he made some new choices. He showed me that it's possible to balance what you want for your home life with what you put into your work. He's a living role model. A real family man. I was with him and his family last week at the annual Business Awards dinner at the Ritz. I was proud he got the Salesman of the Year award for an important Colombian contract, and it was great to see his family sharing the experience with him.

"Then there was Paul. Sadly, I missed a real opportunity with him. He was a truly inspiring guy. Turns out he had lots of ideas for how to improve our company, but because I never listened to him, I didn't appreciate what he had to offer IF-Q corporation. There was this great article in Business Week last month about his company. He started it from scratch, and people are queuing up to join him. Apparently it's one of the best places to work in North America.

"One of my biggest lessons came from my son, Bryan. He wrote a paper about society's lack of true respect and caring. He used lots of examples from his own school and, regretfully, from my company. I was shocked and angry at first. Then he helped me to see that the way we were running the company put the system first and that people were suffering as a result. I was proud of him being invited to read his paper to a research group at Oxford. I think he just may be going places.

"Then, darn it if I didn't bump into an old college friend of mine. James had been a teacher—at Bryan's school, actually—but somehow I hadn't seen him to chat for years. We had lost touch—maybe because I was always so busy at work. Anyway, he came along to support Bryan with the Oxford reading, and we got into a conversation about what James himself was doing. He had actually had the courage to leave the teaching profession and go back into the music industry. He'd always been the arty one when we were younger. It was a real surprise to meet up with him again and an even greater surprise when he gave me a copy of the CD that the students in his music school had just released. I have to confess I've been playing it a lot in the car.

"Finally, I'm almost lost for words at the achievements of my sister Mary and her kids, Catherine and Mark. They are always turning up in my office asking me to sponsor their latest project in Africa. Mary looks about ten years younger and certainly seems to have a lot more energy than me. I've promised to visit their clinic in the jungle this year. I guess they'll have a list of things for me to help out with. Well, that will be a new experience. It's been documented, too, by Mark. He's published a great book of photos about the project that helps people appreciate the hardship over there. Yep, I'm pretty glad they opened my eyes. Apparently it's never too late to make a difference."

"So did you yourself identify these steps as a means to effective new-style leadership?" asks the interviewer, keen to hear the answer.

"Well," says Dan, and he begins to fidget uncomfortably as beads of sweat reappear on his brow. "This is going to sound funny, but one day I walked into my office and there was this book lying on my desk. I don't know where it came from. It had a funny-looking cover, and the paper was strange, like nothing I've seen or felt before. The cover only had two letters on it, an I and an F, intertwined in an unusual way. I felt compelled to read it, and once I started I asked my secretary to cancel my appointments for the day. I was enthralled. It had all these ideas in it."

"Who wrote this book?" asks the interviewer, "Can our viewers get it on Amazon?"

"It's by someone called Tashia; that's all it says. And there's something funny about it. It looks like a really old book, but on the inside cover there is a misprint. The publication date is shown as 2025. That doesn't make sense to me. Here, I brought it with me, take a look..."

Dan leans across the coffee table and the interviewer bends her head to join him, indicating to the camera to focus in on the detail of the pages Dan is showing her.

Dan's wife, standing just off-camera, watches proudly while shuffling some brightly-coloured cards from one hand to the other.

In front of TV screens around the world, viewers sit up, recalling conversations and memories—a moonlit children's playground; the sprinkle of late summer fountains; the autumn wind in a grove of young elm trees; the flames of a winter fire; the budding of spring daffodils...

And somewhere at the back of their minds, a quiet voice whispers:

My name is Tashia, may life be all you claim it to be.

Epilogue

"There is a framework, handed down for many generations, which helps us to guide our questioning," says Tashia, "I am amazed that more people do not use it. I know that, when people do, it brings a focus and clarity to many conversations. People have constantly told me how helpful it is, and how they use it to move towards action and solutions more easily."

"Is this a framework that can be shared and adopted by others?" asks Ghoy.

"Undoubtedly. I am convinced this was its intent. Its time is now. It can be one of the ways in which we regenerate our relationships and conversations with others if this land is to become alive and meaningful again. This framework alone can guide us to see new realities for ourselves. Traditionally, this framework has been called GROW, although it always seems to

me that there are two 'O's in the middle of it. We have limited ourselves by the convention of existing language in giving it a label. Perhaps there is a new name out there somewhere for it – meantime, I shall explain it as it is currently known to this generation.

"It's like a five-pointed star," says Tashia, glancing up at the night sky. "As if it has been sent as a guide for us to live in a new way." As she talks, Tashia strolls to the edge of the circle and picks up an old hazel branch, dry and brittle with time. She returns to the dusty centre of the circle and scratches a star symbol in the dirt.

"It's so simple, some people think it's like magic," she whispers as she starts to explain the five points of the star.

"G is for goal. It's about questions, which help the other create a picture of what they want, to envision success, to set a clear goal for themselves. I've learned it is worth spending time on this part of the conversation to ensure the other person has real clarity on what they want. Sometimes, that clarity alone, the ability to express their goal or desire, helps them become aware of what they need to do to achieve it.

"R is for reality. It brings into focus how near or far the other person is from their desired goal. Sometimes they realize they are only a small step away from what they seek, at other times they realize they still have a huge mountain to climb. In either case this step helps them to take their bearings.

"O is for opportunities. This is the real magic step. I often ask the other person to imagine they have a magic wand and envision what could be possible. We are so often limited by what

we believe is not possible, when we just need to see things differently. Taking time to explore opportunities helps us to find new pathways to our desires.

"The second O is for obstacles. Often we envision obstacles that are not there, or obstacles we think we can't do anything about. More often than not, the obstacle is actually within us, although we like to blame something outside ourselves as being the limiting factor.

"And finally, W is for creating the will to make something happen. To find the one next step that will truly make a difference.

"In summary, this framework serves to guide our questioning. If we hold it in our mind's eye, our questions will help the other person to identify where they want to get to, where they are now and how they will reach their destination. It is the essence of good questioning to guide people along their chosen path.

"This conversation and questioning framework is for the Future Guides to share with the new community to enable and inspire the future."

"This sounds very powerful," says Ghoy.

"I believe we might call it pure coaching."

About the Author

Aileen Gibb leads conversations that inspire new possibilities for individuals, teams and organizations, enabling new futures to emerge. Her work has taken her from the UK and Europe, to North and South America, the Middle East and as far afield as Kazakhstan. In each community, she discovered that people respond enthusiastically to the discovery of their untapped capacity for listening, questioning and real conversation. She coaches leaders at all levels in organizations, releasing their potential and enabling them to be all they can be. Born in Northeast Scotland, Aileen lives in the majestic Canadian Rockies and can be contacted through her website **www.inspiredfuture.org**.

Acknowledgement of the GROW Framework

The GROW conversation framework is in the public domain and widely used in coaching circles. It is my understanding that it may originate from conversations between some coaches who may have had links to a major Consulting Group, where a similar framework was used as a strategic planning tool for organizations. Sir John Whitmore, one of the founders of today's coaching industry, first published GROW as a coaching tool in his book *Coaching for Performance* (Nicholas Brealey Publishing). I was originally introduced to GROW by Paul Kalinauckis and Ruth Webber, two of my earliest teachers in the field of coaching. I am grateful for this foundation, and for the essential purity and power of GROW as a reference point for my GROoW version of conversations that inspire the future.

CPSIA information can be obtained at www.ICGtesting.com
Printed in the USA
LVOW10s0029141015

458198LV00001B/39/P